All the material in this book was confirmed as accurate at the time of publication.

To Anne, who first introduced me to all things Texas. Special thanks to David Courtney and the incredibly helpful librarians throughout the Lone Star State.—H.A.

To Marc, Rocket, and Gidget—definitely stopping here on the road trip!.—J.T.

Inspiring | Educating | Creating | Entertaining

Brimming with creative inspiration, how-to projects, and useful information to enrich your everyday life, quarto.com is a favourite destination for those pursuing their interests and passions.

Text © 2023 Heather Alexander L.L.C. Illustrations © 2023 Jen Taylor

First published in 2023 by Wide Eyed Editions, an imprint of The Quarto Group. 100 Cummings Center, Suite 265D, Beverly, MA 01915, USA. T +1 978-282-9590 F +1 078-283-2742 www.Quarto.com

The right of Heather Alexander to be identified as the author and Jen Taylor to be identified as the illustrator of this work has been asserted by them in accordance with the Copyright, Designs and Patents Act, 1988 (United Kingdom).

A CIP record for this book is available from the Library of Congress.

ISBN 978-0-7112-7406-8
eBook ISBN 978-0-7112-7407-5

The illustrations were created digitally
Set in Quicksand and Thirsty Script

Published by Georgia Amson-Bradshaw and Debbie Foy
Designed by Myrto Dimitrakoulia
Edited by Hattie Grylls
Production by Dawn Cameron

Manufactured in Guangdong, China TT112022

9 8 7 6 5 4 3 2 1

MIX
Paper from responsible sources
FSC® C016973

Only in
TEXAS

Written by **Heather Alexander** · Illustrated by **Jen Taylor**

WIDE EYED EDITIONS

Contents

Welcome to Texas

We're going on a weird, wonderful, and wacky road trip around Texas, where everything is big, **bigger, biggest!** Hop in our (imaginary) pickup truck and let's hit the open road 'cause everything you could ever want is within the borders of this ginormous state. We'll visit ranches and rodeos, enjoy bayous and beaches, and walk through farmland, flower fields, and forests. We'll climb up mountains and into canyons, cross vast deserts and rolling prairies, shop in small towns and gleaming cities. We'll ride horses, paddle down rivers, cheer for touchdowns, eat delicious food, and meet the friendliest folks around. It's no wonder Texas pride is off the charts! As we travel, keep an eye out for some of the offbeat, amazing, and just-plain-weird history, buildings, attractions, festivals, plants, animals, and people that make Texas so unique.

EL PASO

BIG BEND NATIONAL PARK

HOW BIG IS TEXAS? IT'S SO BIG . . .
It takes up 7.4% of the nation's total area!
15 of the 50 states could fit inside it!
El Paso is closer to California than it is to the Gulf Coast!

PANHANDLE

PERMIAN
BASIN

DALLAS

FORT
WORTH

PINEY
WOODS

HILL COUNTRY

AUSTIN

HOUSTON

SAN
ANTONIO

GULF COAST

Where is the true heart of Texas? The GEOGRAPHIC CENTER—an imaginary point that divides the state into four equal areas—lies between the small cities of Brownwood and Brady.

Unlike some other states' square or rectangular outlines, the SHAPE of Texas is unmistakable.

Art is everywhere! Amazing MURALS and colorful street art decorate the most unexpected places.

One of Austin's nicknames is "The City of the Violet Crown," because of its amazing PURPLE SUNSETS. Another nickname is "Silicon Hills" because of the many TECH FIRMS.

Why does the city have a bronze statue of ANGELINA EBERLY in her nightgown shooting a cannon? One night in 1842, Sam Houston (president of the Republic of Texas) and his men secretly tried to move the state capital to Houston by sneaking boxes of historical documents out of Austin. Eberly raced from her bed and fired a cannon, scaring them off. Austin stayed the capital. Yay, Angelina!

The COLORADO RIVER winds through Austin.

On the last Saturday in April, Austin celebrates the donkey from the Winnie-the-Pooh books at EEYORE'S BIRTHDAY PARTY with colorful costumes and, of course, live music.

Austin

Austin is the perfect first stop on our quirky road trip, 'cause this city is known for being weird. And we love that! Austin is the state capital, and it's also called the live music capital of the world. With over 250 live music venues, you can listen (and sing along) to indie, rock, blues, country, jazz, pop, or whatever tunes you love. Are you hungry? Look at all the food trucks lined up! We're fixin' to get out, grab a bite (or two), and dance until bedtime!

Austin is the only city in the world to have super tall MOONLIGHT TOWERS that light up at night. Each Christmas, the tower in Zilker Park gets transformed into a twinkling tree.

The dome of the pink granite CAPITOL BUILDING stands 14.67 feet higher than the nation's Capitol in Washington, D.C.

Austin has the LARGEST URBAN BAT COLONY in North America. On summer evenings, about 1.5 million Mexican free-tailed bats fly out from under the Congress Avenue Bridge in search of food.

Hungry? There are well over a thousand FOOD TRUCKS throughout the city. Yummy BREAKFAST TACOS are the most popular order.

KEEP AUSTIN WEIRD! Austin's unofficial slogan started when a local librarian used the phrase on a radio show in 2000.

Stats and Facts

FAST FACTS

ABBREVIATION: TX

CAPITAL: Austin

STATEHOOD: December 29, 1845, 28th state

NUMBER OF COUNTIES: 254—more than any other state! The founders created many small counties so no one was more than a day's ride on horseback from their courthouse.

POPULATION: Around 30 million. It's the second most populous state (California's first).

AREA: 268,596 square miles. It's the second-largest state (Alaska's first) in total area.

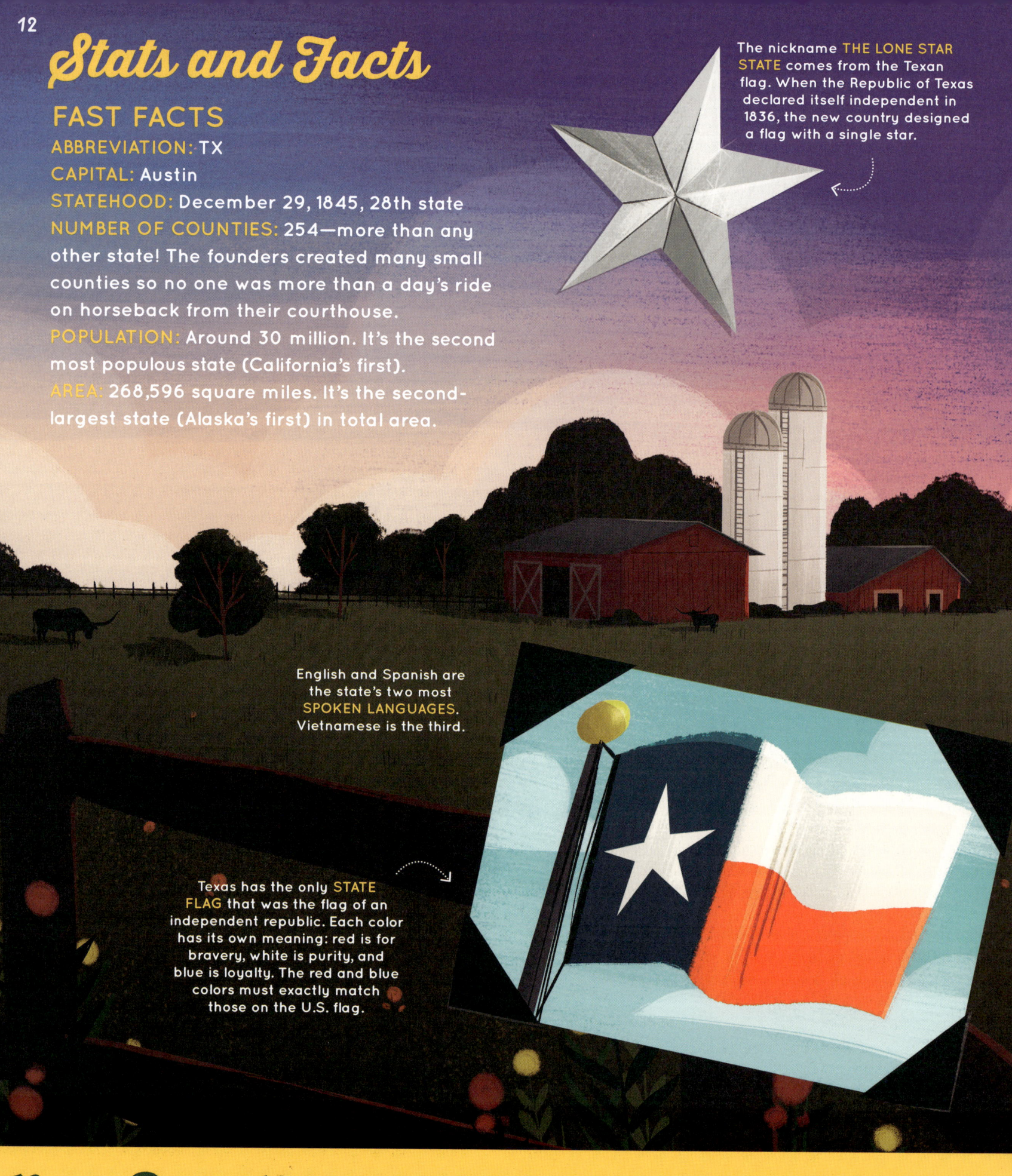

The nickname THE LONE STAR STATE comes from the Texan flag. When the Republic of Texas declared itself independent in 1836, the new country designed a flag with a single star.

English and Spanish are the state's two most SPOKEN LANGUAGES. Vietnamese is the third.

Texas has the only STATE FLAG that was the flag of an independent republic. Each color has its own meaning: red is for bravery, white is purity, and blue is loyalty. The red and blue colors must exactly match those on the U.S. flag.

Next-Door Neighbors

NORTH: New Mexico, Oklahoma, Arkansas   **WEST:** New

HOW DID TEXAS GET ITS NAME?

It's said the Caddo people greeted Spanish settlers with "Taysha," a word for friend that was written down in Spanish as "Tejas" and then in English as "Texas." So it's only fitting that the state motto is "FRIENDSHIP."

IN THE NATION, TEXAS HAS (OR PRODUCES) THE MOST:

- Cattle
- Cotton
- Farms and ranches
- Hay
- Oil
- Sheep (and wool)

STATE SUPERLATIVES

- King Ranch in Kingsville is the country's largest RANCH. At about 1,289 square miles, it's bigger than the state of Rhode Island.
- The Texas State Capitol building in Austin is the nation's largest (but not tallest) STATE CAPITOL.
- The San Jacinto Monument in Houston is the world's tallest MONUMENT COLUMN. It's 13 feet taller than the Washington Monument in Washington D.C.
- Bracken Cave just outside San Antonio has the largest known North American BAT COLONY with over 20 million bats. That's equal to the human population of New York.
- Padre Island is the world's longest BARRIER ISLAND.
- Phantom Springs Cave is believed to be the nation's DEEPEST UNDERWATER CAVE.
- The Tyler Municipal Rose Garden is the country's largest ROSE GARDEN with over 38,000 rosebushes.
- Fasten your seat belt! A stretch of State Highway 130 between Austin and San Antonio has the country's fastest SPEED LIMIT—85 miles per hour.
- The Katy Freeway is the world's widest FREEWAY at 26 lanes across.
- The Texas Rangers are the oldest STATE LAW ENFORCEMENT AGENCY.
- Loving County is the U.S. COUNTY with the fewest people—less than 100.

exico, Mexico   SOUTH: Mexico, Gulf of Mexico   EAST: Oklahoma, Arkansas, Louisiana, Gulf of Mexico

Houston

We're about to blast off for an out-of-this-world adventure in Houston, otherwise known as Space City. The largest city in Texas and fourth largest in the nation, Houston is home to the Johnson Space Center (JSC), where the National Aeronautics and Space Administration (NASA) commands manned space missions and the American portion of the International Space Station. It's also where astronauts come for their two years of rigorous training on land, underwater, and beyond. What do you think? Want to travel to the stars?

The space center was named for U.S. president and Texas native LYNDON B. JOHNSON. Fun fact: Everyone in his family had the initials LBJ. Even their dog was named Little Beagle Johnson.

"Houston, we've had a problem here." After those famous words were received from the damaged APOLLO 13 on April 13, 1970, Mission Control jumped into action, rescuing the spacecraft and its crew.

So close, you could touch them! Space Center Houston, the visitor center of JSC, has the world's largest collection of MOON ROCKS on public display. They're protected in a special clean room.

MISSION CONTROL is very busy whenever a crew is in space. On July 20, 1969, Apollo 11 astronauts Neil Armstrong and Buzz Aldrin became the first people to WALK ON THE MOON, and JSC planned and coordinated the lunar landing.

Houston has lots of hot, steamy days. Luckily there are miles of air-conditioned TUNNELS underneath the downtown streets for people walk through to reach restaurants, stores, office buildings, and hotels.

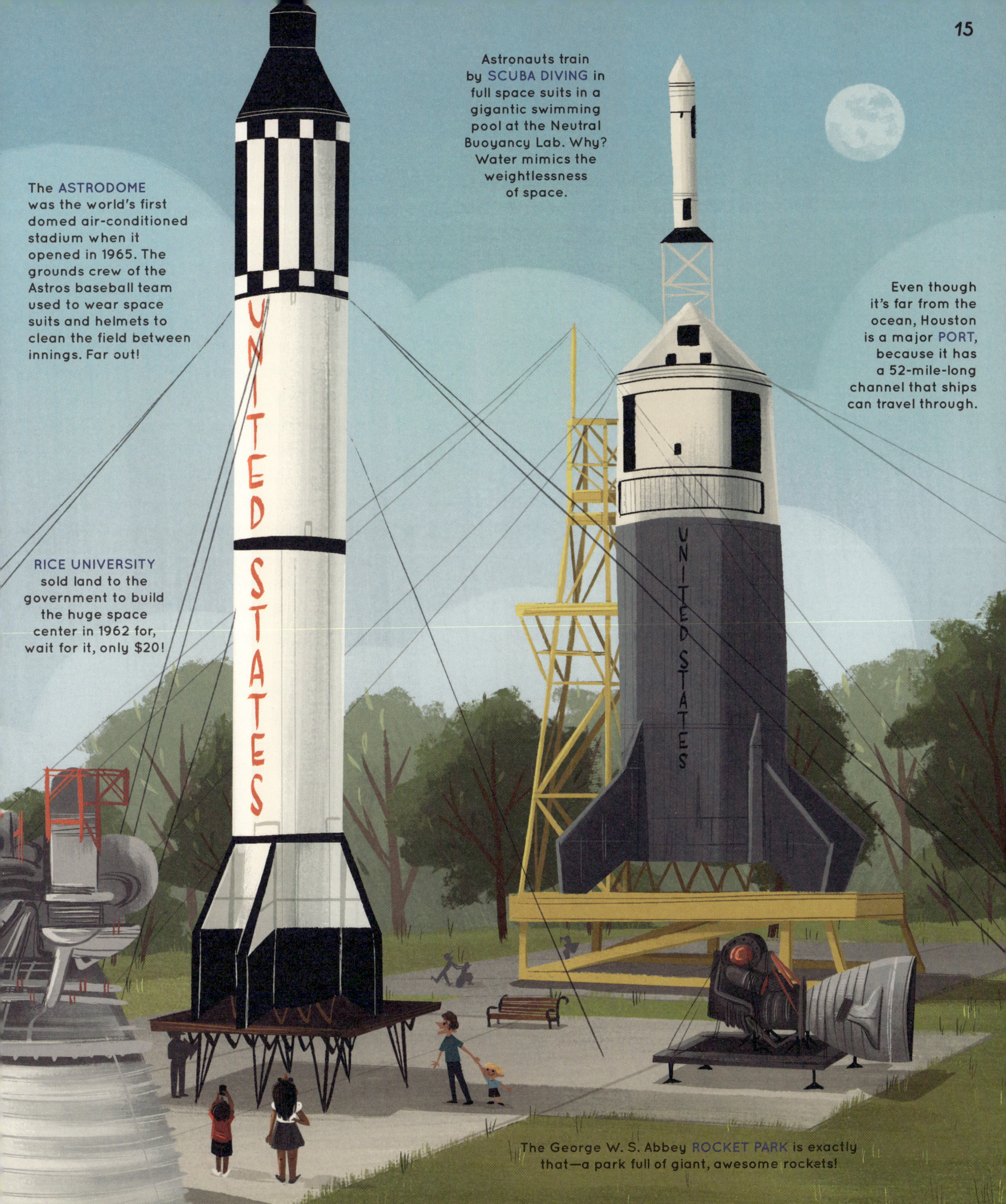

Astronauts train by SCUBA DIVING in full space suits in a gigantic swimming pool at the Neutral Buoyancy Lab. Why? Water mimics the weightlessness of space.

The ASTRODOME was the world's first domed air-conditioned stadium when it opened in 1965. The grounds crew of the Astros baseball team used to wear space suits and helmets to clean the field between innings. Far out!

Even though it's far from the ocean, Houston is a major PORT, because it has a 52-mile-long channel that ships can travel through.

RICE UNIVERSITY sold land to the government to build the huge space center in 1962 for, wait for it, only $20!

UNITED STATES

UNITED STATES

The George W. S. Abbey ROCKET PARK is exactly that—a park full of giant, awesome rockets!

History Timeline

225-65 million years ago
Dinosaurs roamed! Fossils from 21 different species—including *Tyrannosaurus rex*—have been found in Texas.

16,000-20,000 years ago
Earliest evidence of humans living in what is now Texas. Before the Europeans arrived, dozens of indigenous peoples lived across the region, including the Caddo, Karankawa, Atakapa, Coahuiltecan, and Jumano peoples. Later the Apache, Cherokee, Chickasaw, Comanche, Kickapoo, Shawnee, and Wichita peoples arrived.

1519 Spanish sea captain Alonso Álvarez de Piñeda maps the Gulf of Mexico coastline.

1845 Texas becomes the 28th state in the United States of America. It is the only state to enter by treaty rather than territorial annexation. This helps to spark the Mexican-American War.

1842 German farmers and craftspeople begin to settle in the Hill Country.

1836 Texan troops defeat the Mexican army in the Battle of San Jacinto in only 18 minutes! On March 2 (Texas Independence Day), Texas becomes its own country with its own flag and constitution.

1845 Baylor University opens, now the state's oldest continually operating university.

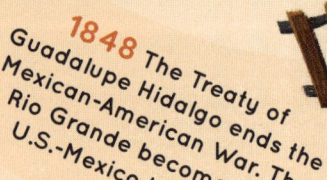

1848 The Treaty of Guadalupe Hidalgo ends the Mexican-American War. The Rio Grande becomes the U.S.-Mexico boundary.

1853 First railroad operates in Texas.

1854 Richard King offers the expert vaqueros of Cruillas, Mexico, jobs on his new huge ranch, jumpstarting the Texas ranching industry.

1861-1865 The Civil War is fought. Texas, where slavery was legal, secedes from the Union and becomes part of the Confederacy.

1961 Henry B. González is the state's first Hispanic U.S. Congress representative.

1957 Raymond Lorenzo Telles Jr. is the first Mexican American elected mayor of a major U.S. city (El Paso).

1953 Dwight D. Eisenhower becomes the first U.S. president born in Texas.

I LIKE IKE

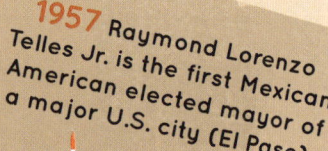

1946 Assault is the only Texas-bred horse to win the racing Triple Crown.

1944 Big Bend National Park is created.

1963 President John F. Kennedy is shot and killed while riding in a car in Dallas. Vice president Lyndon B. Johnson, born in central Texas, is made president.

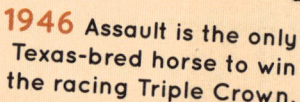

1968 San Antonio hosts the World's Fair.

1969 Mission Control at Johnson Space Center in Houston helps Apollo 11 land on the moon.

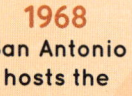

1975 Vietnamese immigrants come to the Gulf Coast after the fall of Saigon, because the climate and fishing industries are similar.

1528 Álvar Núñez Cabeza de Vaca is shipwrecked on Galveston Island and spends eight years with the Native people before going home to Spain.

1682 First permanent European settlement is established by Spain near El Paso.

1685 French explorer René-Robert Cavelier, Sieur de La Salle, sails into East Texas. His colony only lasts a few years.

1718 San Antonio de Valero is one of dozens of missions built by the Spanish throughout Texas as a way to convert Native people to Christianity.

1776 The United States Declaration of Independence is signed.

1836 Two hundred Texans defend the Alamo against the Mexican army led by Antonio López de Santa Anna, but almost all are killed. "Remember the Alamo!" becomes the Texas rallying cry.

1821 Mexico wins its war against Spain for independence, and Texas becomes part of Mexico.

1865 Although President Abraham Lincoln signed the Emancipation Proclamation in 1863, it isn't until June 19, 1865, that the enslaved people of Texas learn they were freed.

1870 Texas is readmitted to the United States.

1874 When the U.S. Army began to forcefully remove the Comanche, Kiowa, Southern Cheyenne, and Arapaho from their longtime Southern Plains homelands, the Native tribes fought back, leading to the Red River War. The army's guns win out, and Native people are forced onto reservations.

1900 The Great Hurricane destroys much of Galveston.

1924 Miriam "Ma" Ferguson becomes the first woman elected governor in Texas.

1910 First U.S. military air flight takes place in San Antonio.

1901 The discovery of oil at Spindletop near Beaumont starts the oil boom.

1988 Houston-resident George H. W. Bush is elected President.

1993 Kay Bailey Hutchison is the first woman from Texas elected to the U.S. Senate.

2000 Former Texas governor George W. Bush is elected president.

2005 Joe Chow of Addison becomes Texas' first Chinese American mayor.

2019 An Truong of Haltom City becomes Texas' first Vietnamese American mayor.

Gulf Coast

We're having a beach day on the Gulf Coast, the 367-mile shoreline bordering the Gulf of Mexico. Inhale salty ocean air as you sink your toes into the soft sand beaches of Galveston, Padre Island, Corpus Christi, and Mustang Island. The waters are so warm, you'll feel like you're swimming in a huge bathtub. The Gulf Coast is the perfect place to dig for sand crabs, search for shells, bike in the breeze, watch dolphins, and eat lots of mouth-watering seafood. Don't forget the sunscreen!

Visit the patients at Sea Turtle, Inc., a SEA TURTLE HOSPITAL in South Padre Island.

Call the Hatchling Hotline during summer to find out when Kemp's Ridley TURTLE BABIES will hatch on the North Padre Island beach. Then watch the tiny turtles scurry into the waves.

Get carried away KITEBOARDING! Balancing on a surfboard, you hold on to a kite and let the wind pull you across the waves. Whoosh!

With its counterclockwise spiral, the LIGHTNING WHELK shell is the official state shell. The whelk is a sea-dwelling snail. It uses its one powerful foot to pry open a clam shell so it can feast on the clam.

The Gulf's warm waters are home to white, pink, brown SHRIMP.

The Gulf Coast is so big it's often called the nation's THIRD COAST.

A 10-mile-long SEAWALL protects Galveston from high tides and storm surges.

The GULF STREAM, which starts in the warm waters of the Gulf of Mexico, is one of the strongest ocean currents in the world. It flows across the Atlantic Ocean and all the way to northern Europe.

Superhighway in the sky! Birds traveling the CENTRAL FLYWAY, a migratory path between Canada and Mexico or Central/South America, use the Gulf Coast as a rest stop.

Enormous steel OIL RIGS pump up petroleum from under the ocean floor. The big rigs employ so many people, they're called "floating cities."

SPECKLED TROUT (specks) and REDFISH (reds) are some of the most desired saltwater catches.

Cast your line at Pirate's Landing Fishing Pier in Port Isabel, the state's longest PIER.

Your family can take SANDCASTLE LESSONS on South Padre Island.

Hang ten to the TEXAS SURF MUSEUM in Corpus Christi to learn about Lone Star wave riders.

Ride the IRON SHARK ROLLER COASTER high above the waves. It has a 100-foot vertical lift then a drop that sends you plunging at 50 miles per hour!

Galveston is on a BARRIER ISLAND, a long narrow strip of sand that sits parallel to the shore.

Spectacular Sports

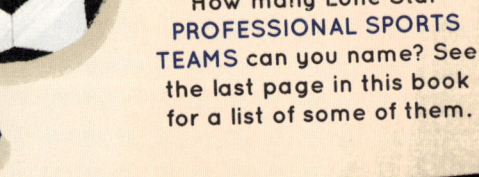

You'll find Texans on fields, courts, and racetracks all across the state. They're also the ultimate fans, cheering super loudly for their favorite athletes and teams.

How many Lone Star **PROFESSIONAL SPORTS TEAMS** can you name? See the last page in this book for a list of some of them.

FOOTBALL and Texas go together like chips and queso. It doesn't matter if it's NFL, college, or high school—football is a way of life.

Some **COLLEGE FOOTBALL** rivalries with wacky names:

Red River Showdown = University of Texas at Austin vs. the University of Oklahoma

Iron Skillet = Southern Methodist University vs. Texas Christian University

Bayou Bucket = University of Houston vs. Rice University

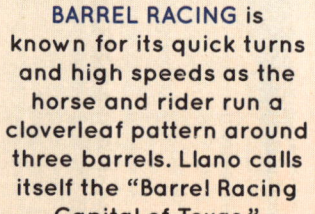

BARREL RACING is known for its quick turns and high speeds as the horse and rider run a cloverleaf pattern around three barrels. Llano calls itself the "Barrel Racing Capital of Texas."

The **HEISMAN TROPHY**, awarded to college football's most outstanding player, was named for John William Heisman, the first full-time coach and athletic director at Rice University in Houston.

RODEO is the official state sport. The West of the Pecos Rodeo started way back in 1883 as a cattle roping competition between two ranch hands.

Born in Brownfield, **SHERYL SWOOPES** was a Texas Tech star, a three-time Olympic gold medalist, and the first player signed to the WNBA, where she was MVP (most valuable player) three times. Wow!

Have a spare minute? Hit the lanes at the International BOWLING Museum and Hall of Fame in Arlington. Bowling is an ancient game—did you know a set was discovered in an ancient Egyptian tomb?

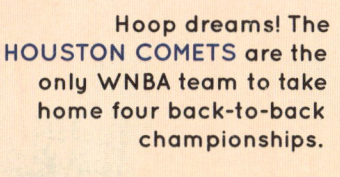

Three cheers for Lawrence Herkimer, inventor of the HERKIE JUMP and the modern pom-pom. Texas Tech, Navarro College, and Trinity Valley Community College boast some of the nation's premier high-flying CHEERLEADING teams.

Hoop dreams! The HOUSTON COMETS are the only WNBA team to take home four back-to-back championships.

The first DANCE DRILL TEAM was created by Gussie Nell Davis at Greenville High School and then at Kilgore College.

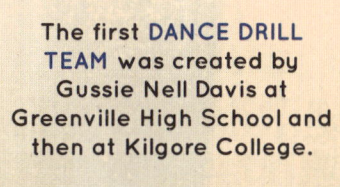

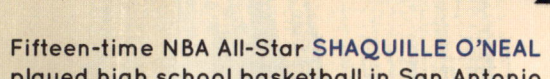

WOMEN'S NATIONAL BASKETBALL ASSOCIATION CHAMPIONS

Vrroom! Houston-born A. J. FOYT is one of the all-time best racers, holding multiple records including 67 IndyCar wins and 7 IndyCar Championships. FORMULA 1 races at Austin's Circuit of Americas, and NASCAR and INDYCAR at Fort Worth's Texas Motor Speedway. Fun fact: 'race car' spelled backward is 'race car'!

Fifteen-time NBA All-Star SHAQUILLE O'NEAL played high school basketball in San Antonio.

While the eagle is the most common MASCOT for Texas high school teams, some schools boast unique cheerleaders:

Abernathy Antelopes
Cuero Gobblers
Frost Polar Bears
Grand Prairie Gophers
Grandview Zebras
Hamlin Pied Pipers
Hutto Hippos
Killeen Kangaroos
Lake Worth Bullfrogs
Mesquite Skeeters
New Braunfels Unicorns
Springtown Porcupines
Trent Gorillas

UNICORNS

San Antonio

We've reached the second-largest city in the state, San Antonio, and its famous Riverwalk or Paseo del Río. The festive, cypress-lined walkway meanders along on both sides of the San Antonio River. Small, stone arched bridges help you cross the water with ease, as mariachi bands play in front of restaurants and shops. At the ten-day Fiesta San Antonio every April, the Riverwalk transforms into an explosion of color. People wear bright clothing, sashes heavy with collectible medals, and hats overflowing with paper flowers. They line the paths decorated with papel picados to enjoy parades and festivities. Viva! Come join the fun!

Glide through the city by WATER TAXI! The native Payaya people called the river Yanaguana, or "refreshing waters."

Every St. Patrick's Day, the river is turned GREEN with an eco-friendly dye and renamed River Shannon, after the river in Ireland.

El Mercado's shopping district is the nations' largest MEXICAN MARKET.

A cross between an Easter egg and a piñata, CASCARONES are brightly colored eggshells filled with confetti. They're cracked over loved ones' heads, and the confetti shower is said to bring good luck.

Can you guess the most visited place in Texas? The ALAMO. Built by Spanish missionaries, the walled fort is famous for the 1836 battle during the Texas revolution.

The MAIN PLAZA dates back to 1731 and is one of the oldest public parks in the U.S.

Keepin' cool! San Antonio is home to the nation's first AIR-CONDITIONED high-rise building, bank, hotel, and Catholic church.

Everything from e-scooters and silverware to diamond rings and laptop computers have been found at the bottom of the river during its periodic CLEANINGS.

ROSITA'S BRIDGE was named in honor of Rosita Fernández, a Mexican American singer who was called "San Antonio's First Lady of Song." The SELENA BRIDGE was named for famed Tejano singer Selena Quintanilla Pérez.

Trees & Flowers

Lone Star trees and flowers give much-needed shade in the brutal summer heat, provide homes for animals, and add a natural pop of color to hills and plains. Did you know Texas was the first state to plant flowers alongside the state highways? Pretty, pretty nice!

No flower says Texas more than the state flower, the BLUEBONNET. Many think the shape of its petals resemble sunbonnets. Every year, the Official State of Texas Bluebonnet Festival is held in Chappell Hill.

PECAN is the state tree and pecan pie is the state pie. But did you know pecans aren't nuts? They're drupes: a fruit with a stone pit (like a peach). What you eat when you eat a pecan is the pit (not like a peach).

The country's largest JUJUBE tree, also called Chinese date tree, stands 45 feet tall at the Fort Worth Botanic Garden. Its small fruit has a sweet apple-like taste.

The LOBLOLLY PINE's name came from a slang word for the lumpy porridge once served to English sailors. In 1971, loblolly seeds traveled to the moon on board Apollo 14. Later, these "moon seeds" were planted around the country, including some at the White House.

Native tribes and settlers crossing Texas were happy to spot a COTTONWOOD tree, because that meant water was nearby.

You can eat both the pads and the many-seeded fruit of the PRICKLY PEAR CACTUS, the state plant. Just be sure to remove the spines!

The purple flowers of the TEXAS MOUNTAIN LAUREL smell like grape Kool-Aid. Really!

We're not sure who named the TEXAS REDBUD, because its flowers are pink-purple. Denton calls itself the "Redbud Capital of Texas."

The MEXICAN HAT FLOWER resembles a broad-brimmed sombrero.

Early pioneers would stuff their mattresses with dried TICKSEED (also called Coreopsis) flowers to help repel fleas and bedbugs.

Can you guess why the AMERICAN BASKETFLOWER is also called the Shaving Brush?

The mighty TREATY OAK in Austin is the sole survivor of the Council Oaks, a grove of 14 live oak trees that was a sacred Native meeting place. According to legend, Stephen F. Austin signed a boundary treaty between his settlers and the Tonkawa and Comanche under its branches.

Hill Country

Flowers, flowers everywhere! We're in the Hill Country, the heart of Texas. The land is rugged but not very high in elevation, which means lots of hills (obviously), as well as crystal clear springs and limestone canyons. Every spring, rainbows of wildflowers blanket the rolling hills. In fact, over 5,000 species of wildflowers bloom in Texas. Doesn't that bluebonnet field over yonder look like the perfect photo spot?

Immigrants from the Czech Republic and Germany brought the POLKA, a fast-paced dance to lively music, with them to Texas. TEJANO MUSIC was then created by combining traditional Mexican music with polka music.

You can hunt for rare blue TOPAZ, the state gem, in Mason County.

Talk about Texas strong! ASHE JUNIPER trees have been growing in the Hill Country for about 125,000 years.

The endangered GOLDEN-CHEEKED WARBLER songbird is found only in the Hill Country and uses Ashe Juniper bark to build its nests.

The feisty GUADALUPE BASS, the official state fish, was once close to extinction but is making a comeback in the Hill Country rivers and streams.

Splash! Jump into the swimming hole at JACOB'S WELL, believed to have the longest underwater cave system in the state.

ENCHANTED ROCK, one of the nation's largest rock formations, is an enormous dome of pink granite.

New Braunfels and Fredericksburg are just a couple of the Hill Country towns founded by GERMAN immigrants. Taste flaky apple STRUDEL at Naeglin's, the oldest bakery in Texas (1868).

Legends say Enchanted Rock is HAUNTED, but scientists say the mysterious creaking sound is the rock cooling as the sun sets. Another legend says spending the night on the rock turns you invisible. Sorry, there's no scientific explanation for that!

The town of Rocksprings says it's the "ANGORA GOAT Capital of the World." Angora goats' fluffy hair, called MOHAIR, is used to make super soft sweaters and socks.

The Hill Country sits on the huge EDWARDS PLATEAU. A plateau is high, flat land.

Museums & Attractions

What's better than high-flying thrills at amusement parks and curious exhibits at museums? When they're amplified by the quirky and unusual!

The Jack Sisemore Traveland RV Museum in Amarillo has the world's OLDEST AIRSTREAM.

Choose your ride! Two FERRIS WHEELS in Dallas lift you high in the sky: the State Fair's Texas Star and the Colony's Grandscape Wheel.

"Howdy, folks!" BIG TEX greets visitors at the annual STATE FAIR OF TEXAS in Dallas. He's the world's tallest cowboy at 55 feet tall and sports a 95-gallon hat. In true Texas style, everything about this fair is big—including its 24-day length!

BARNEY SMITH'S TOILET SEAT ART MUSEUM in The Colony displays 1,400 decorated potty seats. *Oops!* Why is a Saguaro cactus here? Believe it or not, they don't grow in Texas. The prickly pear cactus does.

The very first SIX FLAGS theme park opened in 1961 in Arlington and introduced guests to the log flume and mine train rides. Reach new heights as you swing through the air on the SkyScreamer at Six Flags Fiesta Texas.

Croc your world with a visit to GATOR COUNTRY in Beaumont, an adventure park and sanctuary for alligators, crocodiles, and other reptiles. You can even hold a baby gator.

Slip, slide, and splash on the Master Blaster, an UPHILL WATERSLIDE at New Braunfels' **Schlitterbahn Waterpark** ("slippery road" in German). The Kalahari Resort in Round Rock is home to the nation's largest INDOOR WATER PARK.

Everyone can play at MORGAN'S WONDERLAND in San Antonio! The world's first special needs–focused fun park has over 25 wheelchair-accessible attractions and rides.

No one will die from boredom at the NATIONAL MUSEUM OF FUNERAL HISTORY in Houston. There's even a collection of hearses!

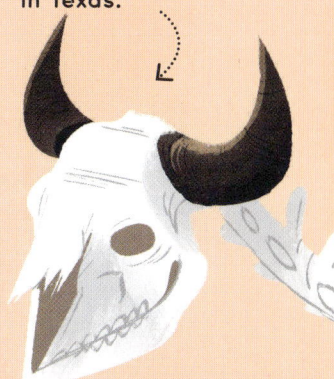

The Panhandle-Plains Historical Museum is the LARGEST HISTORY MUSEUM in Texas.

Get salty at the SALT PALACE MUSEUM in Grand Saline, where the walls are made from salt blocks!

The AMERICAN QUARTER HORSE Hall of Fame & Museum in Amarillo celebrates the popular horse breed used on ranches. The quarter horse got its name because it can outrun other horse breeds in quarter-mile (or less) races.

Love video games? At the NATIONAL VIDEOGAME MUSEUM in Frisco, you can learn the history and play some cool retro ones.

Every holly jolly day is Christmas at the SANTA CLAUS MUSEUM in Columbus!

The FORT WORTH ZOO opened in 1909, with one lion, two bear cubs, an alligator, a coyote, a peacock, and a few rabbits. It's the oldest continuously operational zoo in Texas.

On the banks of the Rio Grande, the LAREDO WATER MUSEUM dives deep into the importance of conserving our fragile resource.

Big Bend National Park

You know how Texas does everything big? Well, the same goes for national parks. At 801,163 acres, Big Bend National Park is bigger than a whole other state (Rhode Island, of course). We're a loooong way from civilization out here. In the state's southwestern corner, Big Bend is one of the most remote national parks in the country. But that means big fun as we explore the rugged wilderness, deep canyons, towering Chisos Mountains, and vast Chihuahuan Desert. Plus the park has more types of birds, bats, butterflies, ants, and scorpions than any other national park—and that's a big deal!

Star gazing is out of sight! The park is an INTERNATIONAL DARK SKY PARK and has the darkest measured skies in the lower 48 states.

Many fossils have been found in the park, including a giant flying PTEROSAUR and the skull of the horned CHASMOSAURUS.

The CONENOSE BUG is also called the kissing bug, vampire bug, or assassin bug, because it likes to suck your blood . . . at night!

Take me to the river! The RIO GRANDE RIVER forms the boundary between Mexico and Big Bend National Park. The park got its name because the Rio Grande makes a U-shaped turn— or a big bend.

Do the twist! The TEXAS MADRONE tree has bright red peeling bark and super twisty branches.

KAYAKERS enjoy the rapids and RAFTERS like to float downriver through the towering, limestone cliffs of Santa Elena Canyon.

Big Bend boasts 450 reported species of BIRDS. It's the only place in the country to see the COLIMA WARBLER, but you'll need to hike uphill for a full day in the hot sun to spot one atop the Chisos Mountains!

The park's Chisos Mountains are called SKY ISLANDS because the tall peaks are surrounded by flat desert.

During summer, thousands of LADYBUGS gather on the high mountain peaks in a red-and-black swarm.

Furry TEXAS BROWN TARANTULAS have eight eyes! Tarantulas are the largest, heaviest, and longest-living spiders in the world.

LECHUGUILLA, a spiny plant sometimes used to make rope, is an INDICATOR SPECIES of the Chihuahuan Desert. So if you were randomly dropped beside this shrub, you'd know exactly where you were because it only grows in the Chihuahuan Desert.

COYOTES can leap up to 14 feet and reach 40 miles per hour in a sprint. Coyotes run with their tails down, while wolves run with their tails straight out, and dogs with their tails up.

Hot tub time! In a section of the Rio Grande known as LANGFORD HOT SPRINGS, the mineral-rich, crystal clear water stays near 105°F.

The GREATER ROADRUNNER's large body makes it hard for it to fly for more than a few moments. Not a problem! The swift bird can run at speeds of 26 miles per hour— that's faster than an e-scooter.

Food, Glorious Food

Texas is a foodie paradise, and its most popular dishes and delicious flavors reflect the diverse groups who've made the state their home.

TEX-MEX is a mix of northern Mexican food and Texas cooking. Tex-Mex uses flour tortillas, plenty of yellow cheese, ground beef, and the spice cumin.

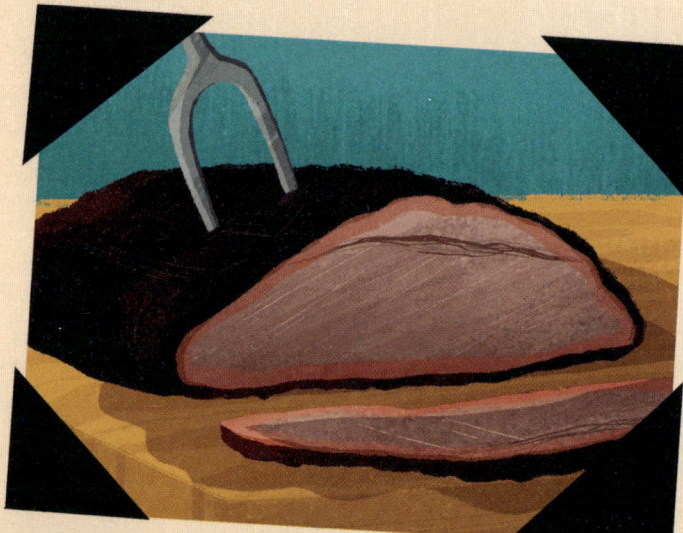

There's no place like Texas for **BARBECUE**. There are so many finger-lickin' ways to eat it: grilled, slow-smoked, brisket chopped with sauce on a bun, and barbacoa, traditionally made from a cow's head or tongue.

CHILE CON QUESO's melted yellow cheese goodness is more popular than pizza. Queso competitions are called quesoffs!

Called "Bowl o' Red," true Texas **CHILI** never ever has beans—just beef, chili peppers, and a few other spices. End of story. In fact, beans are forbidden at the famous Terlingua International Chili Championship.

Czech out **KOLACHES**! The sweet fruit-filled pastry was introduced to Central Texas by immigrants from what is now the Czech Republic. March 1 is National Kolache Day!

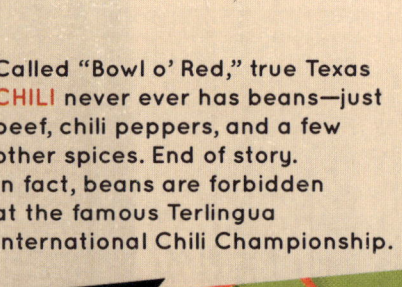

Summer is all about **BLUE BELL ICE CREAM**. In 1907, the Brenham Creamery Company started off by making butter, but a few years later began churning ice cream. Their most popular flavor is still Homemade Vanilla. What's your favorite?

The flavor of BIG RED, a soft drink created in Waco in 1937, has been compared to everything from bubblegum to cotton candy.

There's zero chicken in CHICKEN-FRIED STEAK! The steak cutlet, coated with flour and panfried just like you'd fry chicken, is served with white gravy and mashed potatoes.

Spread the love with HOT PEPPER JELLY, first invented in Lake Jackson in the 1970s. Texans add it to anything and everything.

Deep-fried RATTLESNAKE tastes similar to a very bony white fish.

When Harmon Dobson opened his first WHATABURGER restaurant in 1950 in Corpus Christi, his goal was to make a burger that took two hands to hold and tasted so good you'd take a bite and say, "What a burger!" Well done, Harmon.

The wide, flat chocolate TEXAS SHEET CAKE is made with two favorite Lone Star ingredients: pecans and buttermilk.

TEXAS TOAST got its start at the Pig Stand restaurant in Beaumont in 1941 when a super-thick bread slice wouldn't fit into the toaster. One of the cooks buttered both sides, put it on a griddle, and created the perfect toast for sopping up creamy gravy!

'Tis the season for TAMALES! Corn husk packets stuffed with corn masa and meat (or beans) are a Christmas Eve tradition. Families gather in kitchens for tamaladas, or tamale-making parties.

Stand BÁNH MÌ! The warm, toasty Vietnamese sandwiches are packed with grilled meats and pickled veggies.

El Paso/Ciudad Juárez are TWIN CITIES. Every day people cross the border in both directions to go to work, go to school, and do many other things. El Paso is the country's second-busiest international crossing point. Other twin cities along the Rio Grande are Laredo/Nuevo Laredo and Brownsville/Matamoros.

El Paso is called SUN CITY, because it has about 300 days of sunshine a year.

Pull on your COWBOY BOOTS, the official state footwear! With so many boot makers in town, El Paso calls itself the "Boot Capital of the World."

El Paso

The sun is shining brightly as we follow the curve of the Rio Grande or Río Bravo del Norte into El Paso at the far western tip of Texas. El Paso used to be called El Paso del Norte (the Pass of the North) because its valley was the best (and really only) way for wagons to travel through the surrounding Franklin Mountains. The river acts as a natural border between El Paso in the United States and Ciudad Juárez in Mexico, and Mexico's rich culture colors everything in El Paso, from its architecture to its food and celebrations.

Hop on board a STREETCAR for a ride through town. Back in the 1880s, the streetcars were pulled by mules. The most popular mule was named Mandy.

Since 1935, El Paso has hosted the SUN BOWL, the nation's oldest postseason college football bowl game.

A gigantic STAR (over 400 feet long and 300 feet wide) on the side of the Franklin Mountains is lit up by more than 400 light bulbs. It's the world's largest human-made illuminated star.

The city is in the TRANS-PECOS region of the state.

The only Old West jail outlaw Billy the Kid ever broke *into* (instead of out of) was SAN ELIZARIO JAIL. He posed as a Texas Ranger to trick a guard into releasing his friend.

HUECO TANKS, a rock basin in the Chihuahuan Desert, has hollows, or huecos, that fill with rainwater. For thousands of years, the Kiowa, Mescalero Apache, Comanche, Tigua, and the people of Isleta del Norte Pueblo gathered here. They left behind wall and cave paintings that tell their stories.

Two TIME ZONES! Most of Texas is on Central Standard Time, but El Paso and Hudspeth counties run on Mountain Standard Time. So if it's 9 a.m. in Austin, it's 8 a.m. in El Paso.

Amazing Animals

Because the state features so many diverse landscapes, it's home to over 142 different species of animals, including some found only in Texas. Meet a few of our favorite feathered, furry, and creepy-crawly friends.

BISON once roamed the Great Plains and were an important food source for Native tribes until ranchers hunted them to near extinction. Today, the Official Texas State Bison Herd lives at Caprock Canyons State Park.

What a copycat! The NORTHERN MOCKINGBIRD, the state bird, can sound like 200 other birds and even mimic frogs, crickets, and sirens.

Pee-ew! That musky stink is coming from the JAVELINA. With its long piglike snout, the javelina may look like a wild boar but it's a peccary. You'll spot them munching juicy prickly pear.

Don't be fooled by its name! NINE-BANDED ARMADILLOS, the official state small mammal, have between 7 and 11 bands on their bodies. Armadillos will leap straight up into the air when surprised—and this surprises their attackers! And female armadillos nearly always give birth to four identical quadruplets!

The BLUE LACY, believed to be a mix of a coyote, greyhound, and scenthound, is the state dog. It was named after the four Lacy brothers from the Hill Country who developed the working dog breed.

Texas has more WHITE-TAILED DEER than any other state. The deer raise their tail like a flag to warn the herd of danger.

Texas is the battiest state in the nation, with the most bat species (33). Meet two of our wacky favorites: the HAIRY-LEGGED VAMPIRE BAT feeds on the blood of birds and the GHOST-FACED BAT has a very spooky face.

The mini dinosaur–like TEXAS HORNED LIZARD, also known as the Horny Toad, is the state reptile. Don't mess with them! When angry or frightened, they squirt streams of blood from the corners of their eyes.

When the male TEXAS SPINY LIZARD feels threatened by another male, it starts a push-up contest! They'll both do push-ups until one gives up and runs away.

The goose-looking BLACK-BELLIED WHISTLING DUCK doesn't quack. It whistles. Loudly. They nest inside hollow coastal trees.

The BLACK-TAILED JACKRABBIT can jump up to 20 feet in a single bound (the length of a backyard trampoline) and runs in a zigzag pattern when trying to escape predators. Pretty tricky!

Found in the Rio Grande Valley, CHACHALACAS (say that three times fast!) are named for their screaming, early morning cha-cha-lac-a calls.

Creme Puff from Austin was the OLDEST CAT on record, living a whopping 38 years. His owner fed him turkey bacon and eggs every morning. Guess breakfast really is the most important meal of the day!

The endangered TEXAS BLIND SALAMANDER only lives in water-filled caves in Hays County. Because it stays in total darkness and has no need to see, its eyes are just two black spots underneath its skin.

The book, movie, and TV show *FRIDAY NIGHT LIGHTS* was based on one of Odessa's high school football teams.

In the 1950s, archaeologists discovered the fossilized remains of a prehistoric woman on the Scharbauer Ranch in Midland County. They called her MIDLAND MINNIE.

WEST TEXA

HOME 20 0

TOUC

TEXAS OIL

Stadiums boast high-definition JUMBOTRON display boards to match the schools' jumbo-sized pride.

MIDLAND was originally named Midway because it was the midway point between Fort Worth and El Paso on the Texas and Pacific Railway in 1881. Now its nickname is "Tall City," because of its skyscrapers.

Halftime heroes! The Texas award-winning MARCHING BANDS are always some of the finest in the country. The band's leader is called the DRUM MAJOR, even when they don't play the drums.

IGH SCHOOL
VISITOR
17 17

DOWN

The Permian Basin is the heart of oil country. PERMIAN was a geologic time period so long ago (299 million years ago) that there was only one continent on Earth, called Pangaea.

Massive homecoming MUMS—arrangements of chrysanthemums, ribbons, and lights—are a Lone Star tradition. A mum-maker (yep, that's a job) in Corpus Christi created a mum in 2021 that's taller than Big Tex!

STADIUM

The PETROLEUM MUSEUM in Midland has the world's largest collection of antique oil drilling equipment.

Midland is the former home of PRESIDENTS George H. W. Bush and George W. Bush, and former First Lady Barbara Bush.

Oil or petroleum is often called BLACK GOLD. Oil is measured in BARRELS. One barrel = 42 gallons. (A big jug of milk holds one gallon.)

Permian Basin

We're rolling into the Permian Basin on a fall Friday night and that means one thing: high school football under lights seen from miles away. Workers have left the oil fields, and the stadiums are packed with fans young and old. Can you hear the applause? Marching bands play, color guards twirl, and cheerleaders tumble. The passion here—and all over Texas—for high school football is bigger than the state itself. Let's find a seat 'cause the home team just intercepted the ball and . . . touchdown!

Cool Inventions

Dream big and embrace the new, the incredible, and the never-been-seen-before. Here are just a few of the many inventions from the innovative Lone Star State.

DR PEPPER (never put a period after the Dr) was invented by pharmacist Charles Alderton in Waco in 1885. The recipe is so top secret that it's been split into two halves, kept in safety deposit boxes in two different banks.

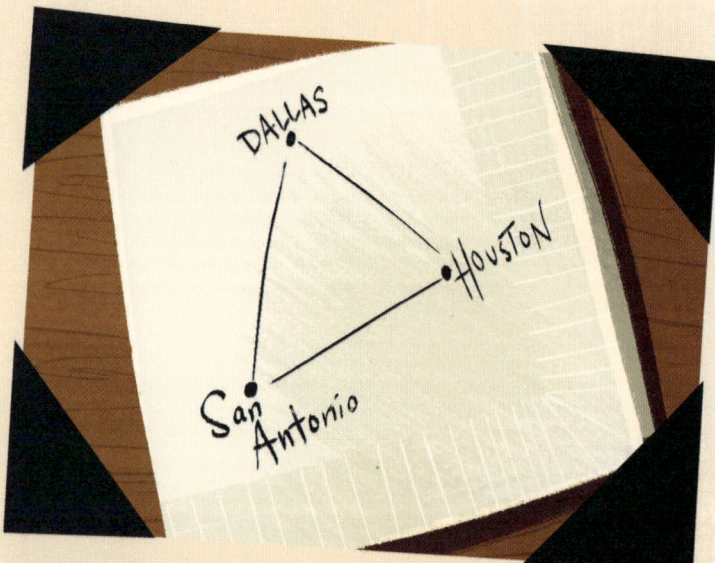

In 1982, at a House of Pies in Houston, three engineers sketched a design for a portable personal computer on the back of a placemat. This idea became **COMPAQ** computers.

SOUTHWEST AIRLINES got its start on a napkin! In 1967, Herb Kelleher and Rollin King drew a triangle with three lines showing how they'd fly between Dallas, Houston, and San Antonio.

In 1984, Michael Dell started a billion dollar tech company, **DELL** computers, in his University of Texas dorm room.

The integrated circuit computer chip, or **MICROCHIP**, was invented by Jack Kilby of Texas Instruments in Dallas in 1958. Without it, there wouldn't be laptop computers or cell phones. He also invented the first pocket-sized **CALCULATOR**.

In 1978, John Mackey and Renee Lawson Hardy borrowed money to open a small natural foods store in Austin. They lived at the store, using the dishwasher as a shower! Two years later, this became the first **WHOLE FOODS** grocery store.

Inspired by the movie *Star Wars*, George Carter invented LASER TAG and opened the first laser tag arena in Dallas in 1984.

Samuel Bert of Dallas created the first SNOW CONES at the State Fair of Texas in 1919. He later patented the snow cone ice-crushing machine.

7-ELEVEN started in Dallas in 1927, when John Jefferson Green and Joe C. Thompson Jr. began selling milk, eggs, and bread in front of local icehouses. The name came from the long hours their "convenience stops" stayed open: 7 a.m. to 11 p.m.

In 1929, the discovery of a red grapefruit growing on a pink grapefruit tree in the Rio Grande Valley led to the creation of the sweet RUBY RED GRAPEFRUIT, the official state fruit.

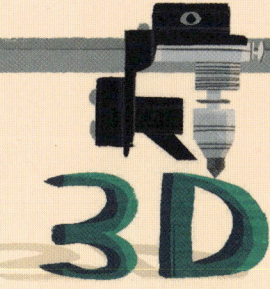

3D PRINTING started in the early 1980s at the University of Texas at Austin with a process called selective laser sintering.

FRITOS curly corn strips were invented in 1932 in San Antonio by Charles Doolin. FRITO PIE, a popular concession stand snack, is made by filling the chip bag with chili, cheese, and often onions.

America's first food truck! The CHUCK WAGON was invented in 1866 by Charles Goodnight to carry cooking equipment and food (mostly beans, salted meats, and biscuits) for cattle drives.

The HENNESSEY VENOM F5, made in Sealy, is one of the world's fastest cars. It has clocked speeds over 300 miles per hour!

The COMANCHE once called this area home.

PALO DURO CANYON, the nation's second-largest canyon (after the Grand Canyon in Arizona), plunges into the flatlands like an upside-down mountain range. The red-rock canyons are perfect for hiking and horseback riding.

Early settlers built WINDMILLS to pump underground water for livestock and people, because there was little surface water. Take a spin at the American Windmill Museum in Lubbock.

Did you know one beef COW poops about 15 times a day and produces about 22,000 pounds of manure each year?

Hungry? At the Big Texan Steak Ranch and Brewery, the meal is free if you can finish their enormous 72-ounce STEAK plus all the sides in less than an hour!

Panhandle

An endless sky is calling! As we cruise across the superflat Texas Panhandle, the open road and blue sky feel as if they go on forever and ever. Any guess on how the Panhandle got its name? The state's straight and narrow northern part sticks out, looking just like the handle of a pot or pan! This is a region of natural wonders, short-grass prairies, longhorns and pronghorns, and heaps of roadside oddities along historic Route 66.

It's believed the city of AMARILLO (Spanish for yellow) was named for the yellow soil on the creek banks. In the early days, the houses in town were painted yellow.

The TEXAS OUTDOOR MUSICAL is performed during summertime sunsets beneath a 600-foot cliff at Palo Duro Canyon State Park.

LLANO ESTACADO is one of the nation's largest MESAS, a flat-topped hill with steep sides. Settlers thought the landform looked like a tabletop, so they named it *mesa*, which means "table" in Spanish.

Lubbock is the hometown of 1950s rock 'n' roller BUDDY HOLLY.

Bring a can of spray paint to graffiti the cars at CADILLAC RANCH, a row of 10 Cadillac cars stuck nose-first into the ground. Supposedly they're buried at the same angle as the Great Pyramid of Giza in Egypt!

TEXAS
US
66

The PRONGHORN is the only animal in the world with horns that branch. It's also the world's fastest herbivore, clocking speeds of up to 60 miles per hour.

ROUTE 66 runs through the Panhandle. Also called "Main Street of America" and "Mother Road," it was the first major road to connect towns between Chicago, Illinois, and Santa Monica, California, when it was built in the 1920s.

Here come the TUMBLEWEEDS! One strong wind sends this weed (its real name is Russian thistle) rolling, spreading thousands of seeds as it goes.

PRAIRIE DOG TOWN in Lubbock is a sanctuary for black-tailed prairie dogs. These little critters aren't dogs (more like squirrels) and they greet each other with a kiss! By touching noses and locking teeth, they can tell if they're members of the same family group.

Fun Festivals

Texas is overflowing with festivals that are both a little odd and totally awesome (and sometimes a bit of both). From roses to mosquitos to watermelon seed spitting, there's something for everyone!

Brownsville and its Mexican sister town, Matamoros, celebrate CHARRO DAYS. The fiesta starts with a loud traditional Mexican GRITO, or celebratory shout.

Buzz over to the GREAT TEXAS MOSQUITO FESTIVAL in Clute to honor the bloodsucking insect and meet mascot Willie-Man-Chew, a 26-foot-tall mosquito in a cowboy hat and boots.

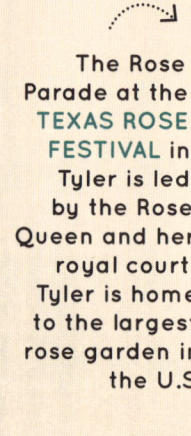

The Rose Parade at the TEXAS ROSE FESTIVAL in Tyler is led by the Rose Queen and her royal court. Tyler is home to the largest rose garden in the U.S.

See how far you can spit at the World Championship Seed Spitting Contest at the LULING WATERMELON THUMP. "Thump" is the sound you hear when you tap a ripe watermelon with your finger.

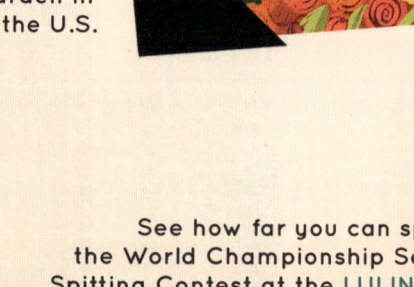

Who's ready to kick up their heels and celebrate Czech heritage at Ennis' NATIONAL POLKA FESTIVAL and WESTFEST in West.

Let your imagination take flight at Austin's ABC KITE FEST.

Isn't it oat-rageous that Bertram Oatmeal Festival has an OATMEAL EATING CONTEST?

Rock and roll! Llano Earth Art Festival hosts the WORLD ROCK STACKING CHAMPIONSHIP, with awards for tallest stack, best balancer, and most rocks in a single tower.

The POTEET STRAWBERRY FESTIVAL is one of the world's biggest berry bashes!

Feeling antsy? A mound of fun awaits at Marshall's FIRE ANT FESTIVAL, including the make-an-ugly-face contest. Could you win that?

FIESTAS PATRIAS in Houston celebrates Mexican Independence Day on September 16 with parades, Tejano music, and dancers from Ballet Folklórico.

Get clucking at the East Texas Poultry Festival's CHICKEN CLUCKING CONTEST.

FAIRY TALES

POEMS

CHAPTER 12

The Texas Book Festival in Austin and the North Texas Teen Book Festival in Irving are all about the LOVE OF READING. We're down for that!

Fort Worth

Hold your horses and kick up your spurs, because we're heading into Fort Worth for a taste of the Old West. Nicknamed "Cowtown," Fort Worth was once the heart of cowhand country and an important rest stop for cattle drives. On a cattle drive, herders on horseback moved thousands of mooing cows from one place to another. At the historic Fort Worth Stockyards, we can still watch cowhands drive a herd of longhorns down East Exchange Avenue! What are you waiting for? Giddyup!

A **TEXAS LONGHORN** named Cowboy Tuff Chex holds the world record for longest horn spread, measuring 8.6 feet—or about the length of a surfboard! The ranchers who bought him at auction in Fort Worth had to purchase an extra wide trailer to drive him home!

BLACK COWBOYS made up about a quarter of the Old West cowboy population.

BILL PICKETT, born in 1870 near Taylor to formerly enslaved parents, was the first Black honoree in the National Rodeo Hall of Fame. He invented the sport of "bulldogging," or wrestling a runing steer.

PAN DE CAMPO is the state bread (yep, there's a state bread). The round, flat biscuit was first made in a **DUTCH OVEN** by vaqueros, and later by cowboys in a cast-iron skillet over a campfire.

"All hat and no cattle" is a Texas saying for someone who is all talk and no action.

Quick, quick, slow, slow. That's how you count the **TEXAS TWO-STEP**. Circle the dance hall floor or try a line dance ... or two.

HORSES have the largest eyes of any land mammal. Their eyes are on the side of their head, letting them see nearly all the way around.

...RTH STOCK YARDS

HOTEL →

The **NATIONAL COWGIRL MUSEUM AND HALL OF FAME** is the only museum in the world that celebrates the legendary women who helped shape the West.

The first **INDOOR RODEO** was held at the Cowtown Coliseum in 1918.

Fort Worth's historic Stockyards Hotel was a hideout for the **OUTLAWS** Bonnie and Clyde.

Established as an army outpost in 1849, Fort Worth was settled on the banks of the Trinity River. Millions of cows were herded from Fort Worth along the **CHISHOLM TRAIL** into Kansas.

MUSEUM

GENERAL STORE

GENERAL STORE

Mexican cattle herders known as **VAQUEROS** ("vaca" means "cow" in Spanish) were the original cowboys, and the wide-brimmed sombreros they wore became the **COWBOY HAT**.

Change Makers

Countless creative and courageous Texans have transformed our world. We choose just a handful of the many influential pioneers, artists, authors, activists, athletes, and leaders to feature. Many were the first from their community to achieve a goal, effect change, or do something super cool.

QUANAH PARKER was the last chief of the Comanche tribe's Kwahadi branch. Born about 1848 near Wichita Falls, he became a full warrior at age 15. When the U.S. government moved the Comanche onto reservations, Parker refused to go. In 1874, he gathered warriors from among the Comanche, Cheyenne, and Kiowa to fight in the Red River War. They held out for a year before surrendering. Texas celebrates Quanah Parker Day on the second Saturday in September.

At the age of 89, retired teacher and Marshall native **OPAL LEE** walked from Fort Worth to Washington, D.C. The two and a half miles she traveled each day represented the time between the formal abolishment of slavery on January 1, 1863, and the day that message reached Black Texans in Galveston: June 19, 1865. In 2021, Juneteenth was declared a federal holiday.

Award-winning singer, songwriter, and actress **BEYONCÉ KNOWLES** was born and raised in Houston. Before her solo career, she was part of the all-female pop R&B group Destiny's Child. Beyoncé holds the record for most Grammys won by a female artist.

Before becoming a best-selling author, San Antonio-native **RICK RIORDAN** worked as a middle-school teacher. His famous series *Percy Jackson and the Olympians* got its start when his son asked for a bedtime story based on Greek mythology. He's also written *The Kane Chronicles*, the Magnus Chase series, and *The Trials of Apollo*—and over 100 million of his books are in print!

SANDRA DAY O'CONNOR was the first woman appointed to the U.S. Supreme Court, the nation's highest court, serving from 1981 until 2006. Born and schooled in El Paso, she worked first as a lawyer before becoming a judge.

BESSIE COLEMAN from Atlanta was the first Black woman and the first woman of Cherokee descent to earn a pilot's license in America. She had to move to France to learn to fly, because no American school would teach her. When she performed her famous aerial tricks in shows across the country.

Born in Rogers, **ALVIN AILEY** performed on Broadway before founding the Alvin Ailey American Dance Theater in 1958. He choreographed 79 ballets and modern dances, often drawing inspiration from church services and local dance hall music. He received the Presidential Medal of Freedom for his contributions to civil rights and dance in America.

Houston's **PAUL "RED" ADAIR** was one of the world's most famous oil well fire fighters. In 1962, he put out a gas fire that had burned for six months in the Sahara Desert, and after the Gulf War, he battled thousands of oil well fires in Kuwait. His nickname came from his red hair, his all-red clothing, and the red cars and trucks he drove.

Country singer and songwriter **WILLIE NELSON**, born in Abbott, got his first guitar at age six and played with a local polka band at age 10. He moved to Austin and began to record and perform his "outlaw" country music, winning 10 Grammys. Every Fourth of July, he hosts a huge picnic-concert and, when he's not singing, he cares for rescued horses on his ranch in Hill Country.

SIMONE BILES is the most decorated gymnast ever with 32 Olympic and world championship medals. Raised by her grandparents in Spring after years in foster care, she started tumbling classes at age six. Four gymnastic moves have been named after her—all called "The Biles." In 2022, she received the Presidential Medal of Freedom.

San Antonio-born **EMMA TENAYUCA** was a Mexican American labor organizer and civil rights activist. She was arrested at age 16 for picketing the Finck Cigar Factory for unfair labor practices and became famous for organizing the Pecan-Shellers' Strike of 1938. Shelling was one of the lowest-paying jobs, and inhaling pecan dust caused serious health problems. She was called "La Pasionaria" ("The Passionate One"), because she stood up for the working poor.

Superstar singer-songwriter Selena Quintanilla Pérez, born in Lake Jackson, was made lead singer of her dad's band at age ten. As a solo singer, she was known simply as **SELENA**, and her beautiful voice popularized Tejano music worldwide. Her life was cut short in 1995, just as she was becoming a superstar.

Born in Port Arthur and raised in Beaumont, **MILDRED "BABE" DIDRIKSON ZAHARIAS** has been called one of the greatest female athletes ever. In 1932, she took home gold and silver Olympic medals in hurdles, javelin, and high jump. She was also a star basketball and baseball player and golfer. She won 82 tournaments and started the Ladies Professional Golf Association.

With the retractable roof enclosed, the entire Statue of Liberty could fit into the stadium (technically in Arlington, not Dallas) where the DALLAS COWBOYS play.

Highland Park Village, developed in 1931, was the first planned SHOPPING CENTER in America.

Join the skyline squad for a 360-degree view of the city on the GeO-Deck at the REUNION TOWER orb, or "The Ball."

Have you seen the 30-foot-tall EYEBALL sculpture in the middle of downtown?

Dallas

It's just a hop, skip, and a jump east to the "Big D." Look at that view, y'all! Dallas's gleaming skyline of skyscrapers is so dazzling it's been voted best in the world. Big-city excitement pulses in the air. The Dallas Arts District, the largest in the country, has nineteen blocks of museums, venues, and galleries. In the mood for some shopping? Well, Dallas offers more shops per person than any other U. S. city. Let's see what the Big D has in store for us!

In 1963, President JOHN F. KENNEDY was assassinated while riding in a convertible car through Dealey Plaza. It's believed the fatal shots were fired from the sixth-floor window of the former Texas School Book Depository. There's now a museum there called the SIXTH FLOOR MUSEUM.

Dallasites reach for Snuffer's CHEDDAR FRIES, dripping with melted cheese, or a cup of ELOTE, boiled corn with crumbled cotija cheese, cream, and butter.

The Neiman Marcus department store, which first opened in 1907 in Dallas, is famous for its Christmas catalog of outrageous FANTASY GIFTS. Would you rather recieve a ten-gallon hat for your dog, your own helicopter, or mermaid swimming lessons?

One of the original copies of the DECLARATION OF INDEPENDENCE is on display at the Dallas Public Library.

A slice of the former president's WEDDING CAKE has been buried in the cornerstone of Woodrow Wilson High School for almost 100 years.

Many legendary blues and jazz musicians, such as Stevie Ray Vaughan and T-Bone Walker, got their start playing in the neighborhood of DEEP ELLUM.

The Galleria Dallas Shopping Mall boasts the country's tallest indoor CHRISTMAS TREE.

The Awe of Mother Nature

Tornadoes, hurricanes, floods, droughts, and extreme temperatures—Mother Nature likes to take the Lone Star State for a spin. But no matter what scary hazard is thrown their way, locals know the secret to staying safe: be prepared. They create plans with their families, gather supplies, pack emergency kits . . . 'cause standing Texas strong is easy when you're ready for anything.

The Great Storm

The GREAT GALVESTON HURRICANE of 1900 was the deadliest natural disaster in U.S. history. The epic storm caused the ocean waves to surge 8–15 feet, leaving the city in ruins and taking between 6,000 and 12,000 lives.

It's called THE GREAT STORM because weather forecasters didn't start naming storms until the 1950s. Under Clara Barton, the American Red Cross raised money to build an orphanage for storm victims by selling photographs of the destruction.

Eye of the Storm

Texas has had more recorded TORNADOES than any other state, with most touching down in the northern Red River Valley. The spring months between 4 and 8 p.m. seem to be the most popular times for a whirl.

Some meteorologists, or weather scientists, are STORM CHASERS. They drive up real close to twisters to learn how they work. Me? I race in the opposite direction!

It's Raining, It's Pouring

In 1979, Tropical Storm Claudette dropped 42 inches of rain on Alvin in just 24 hours! When Hurricane Harvey blew through Port Arthur in 2017, it dumped over 60 inches of rain, setting the record for the nation's HEAVIEST RAINFALL from a tropical cyclone.

Drought It

To battle early 1900s West Texas DROUGHT, C. W. Post (the cereal company founder) tried to give Mother Nature a helping hand. He attached explosives to kites and flew them into the clouds (23 different times!) to ignite rain. His plan sizzled though, and the land stayed dry. A series of blinding dust storms called the DUST BOWL in the 1930s devastated the Panhandle's plains, destroying crops and killing livestock. For years, people endured dust in their beds, on their walls, and in their hair, eyes, and teeth.

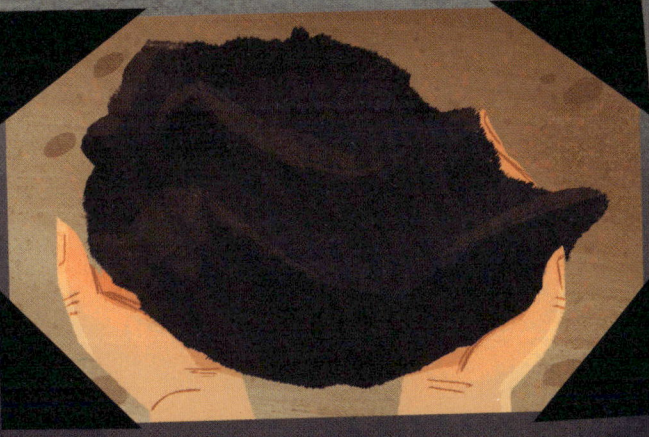

Black Gold

In 1901, an enormous GEYSER OF OIL exploded from a drill site on SPINDLETOP HILL and started the Texas oil boom. The oil spurted higher than an 18-story building! Nobody had ever seen a gusher so powerful and so plentiful. Today, a replica in Beaumont sprays water into the sky.

PETROLEUM is found deep underground and has been there for millions of years. It was formed by fossilized plants and animals buried beneath layers of mud that with heat and pressure turned into petroleum.

Texas is not just fossil fuels. With WIND turbines galore, the state produces the most renewable wind energy in the country.

Rocking It

The Odessa METEOR CRATER, the third-largest in the U.S., formed over 62,000 years ago when nickel-iron meteorites collided with Earth.

The state's largest recorded HAILSTONE fell during a hailstorm in Hondo in 2021. It weighed in at 1.26 pounds—about the same as a jar of peanut butter!

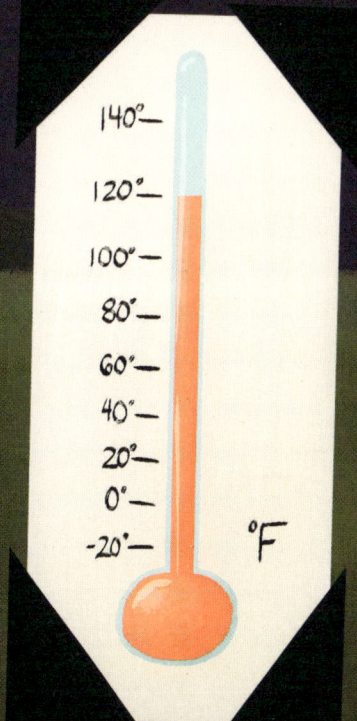

Hot Out Here

Texas temperatures reached 120°F, the HOTTEST on record in the state, in 1936 in Seymour and again in 1994 in Monahans.

Brrr...

During the GREAT BLIZZARD of 1899, people ice-skated on the Brazos River in Waco. On February 12, 1899, Tulia recorded the state's coldest temperature of -23° F.